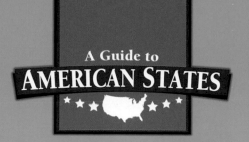

A Guide to
AMERICAN STATES

North Dakota

THE PEACE GARDEN STATE

MEDIA ENHANCED BOOKS
AV²
BY WEIGL
ADDED VALUE • AUDIO VISUAL

www.av2books.com

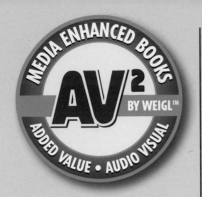

AV² provides enriched content that supplements and complements this book. Weigl's AV² books strive to create inspired learning and engage young minds in a total learning experience.

Your AV² Media Enhanced books come alive with...

Audio
Listen to sections of the book read aloud.

Key Words
Study vocabulary, and complete a matching word activity.

Video
Watch informative video clips.

Quizzes
Test your knowledge.

Go to **www.av2books.com**, and enter this book's unique code.

Embedded Weblinks
Gain additional information for research.

Slide Show
View images and captions, and prepare a presentation.

BOOK CODE

U 8 3 0 5 3 9

Try This!
Complete activities and hands-on experiments.

... and much, much more!

AV² by Weigl brings you media enhanced books that support active learning.

Published by AV² by Weigl
350 5th Avenue, 59th Floor
New York, NY 10118
Website: www.av2books.com   www.weigl.com

Library of Congress Cataloging-in-Publication Data

Watson, Galadriel Findlay.
 North Dakota / Galadriel Watson.
    p. cm. -- (A guide to American states)
Includes index.
ISBN 978-1-61690-806-5 (hardcover : alk. paper) -- ISBN 978-1-61690-482-1 (online)
1. North Dakota--Juvenile literature. I. Title.
F636.3.W383 2011
978.4--dc23
                        2011019028

Printed in the United States of America in North Mankato, Minnesota

052011
WEP180511

Project Coordinator Jordan McGill
Art Director Terry Paulhus

Photo Credits
Every reasonable effort has been made to trace ownership and to obtain permission to reprint copyright material. The publishers would be pleased to have any errors or omissions brought to their attention so that they may be corrected in subsequent printings.

Weigl acknowledges Getty Images as its primary image supplier for this title.

Contents

Competitive events in the state's rodeos showcase riding and wrangling skills. North Dakota has close to 2 million heads of cattle, and modern cowboys continue the traditions of cowboys from the past.

Introduction

American Indians were the first people to inhabit what is now North Dakota. European explorers and fur traders arrived next, followed by settlers. However, the region's geographic isolation has kept the population fairly low. The seemingly endless landscape of hills and prairies provides North Dakotans with plenty of room in which to live.

The state's expansive farmland produces enormous quantities of wheat and other crops. The open spaces are also a destination for tourists who want to escape from overcrowding. Visitors can learn about the state's rich American Indian heritage, follow the paths of famous explorers, and enjoy themselves at beautiful parks.

In southwestern North Dakota, mixed-grass prairies are common. In the northeast, tall-grass prairies are the norm. However, most of the prairies have been turned into farmland.

The sandstone features of the rugged North Dakota badlands have been shaped by the forces of nature. The flat-topped hills of the badlands are called buttes.

The nickname displayed on North Dakota license plates is the Peace Garden State. The saying refers to the International Peace Garden that North Dakota shares with Canada. The state's other nicknames highlight different aspects of its sights and heritage. The nickname Flickertail State refers to the flickertail squirrel. The animal is a familiar sight in North Dakota, flicking its tail as it runs. The Sioux State refers to one of North Dakota's American Indian groups. The Roughrider State comes from the First U.S. Volunteer Cavalry, or Roughriders, who fought in the Spanish-American War under the leadership of Theodore Roosevelt. He was a rancher in North Dakota before becoming president of the United States.

Where Is North Dakota?

North Dakota is located in the north-central part of the United States. The state sits exactly in the middle of the North American continent. In fact, a monument near the town of Rugby marks what is believed to be the continent's geographic center.

The state's land was acquired by the United States in two parts. In 1803 the United States bought the southwestern section from France as part of the Louisiana Purchase. The northeastern part was obtained through a border treaty with Great Britain in 1818.

Farmland covers about 40 million acres of North Dakota.

The majority of in-state railroads in operation are for industrial use, including moving agricultural products.

White Butte is the highest point in North Dakota, at 3,506 feet above sea level. It is located on private property in the southwest part of the state.

The lowest elevation in the state is located in the northeast, in the Red River Valley. That area is 750 feet above sea level. Thousands of years ago, the eastern end of the state was a glacial lakebed.

Of the 50 states, North Dakota is 17th in size, ranked by land area. The state's land area is about 68,976 square miles.

The state straddles two different time zones. Southwestern North Dakota is in the Mountain time zone, while the rest of the state is one hour ahead in the Central time zone.

The state seal contains 42 stars, one for every state in the Union as of 1889, the year when North Dakota, South Dakota, Montana, and Washington were admitted.

Of all the states, North Dakota is considered the most rural. Farms cover about 90 percent of the land.

Before becoming a state, North Dakota was part of the Dakota Territory. This territory also included South Dakota, along with parts of Montana and Wyoming. By the time the Dakota Territory became eligible for statehood, it was clear that the north and the south had developed separately. A railroad ran across the territory from east to west, and people living in the north rarely interacted with people in the south. Each region wanted its own government. On November 2, 1889, North Dakota and South Dakota were admitted to the Union as separate states.

Mapping
North Dakota

North Dakota is bordered by Minnesota to the east, South Dakota to the south, Montana to the west, and the Canadian provinces of Manitoba and Saskatchewan to the north. Two major freeways cross the state. Interstate 94 runs east and west, and Interstate 29 is a major north-south route.

Sites and Symbols

STATE SEAL
North Dakota

STATE BIRD
Western
Meadowlark

STATE FLOWER
Wild Prairie
Rose

STATE FLAG
North Dakota

STATE ANIMAL
Nokota Horse

STATE TREE
American Elm

Nicknames Peace Garden State, Flickertail State, Roughrider State, Sioux State

Motto Liberty and Union, Now and Forever, One and Inseparable

Song "North Dakota Hymn," words by James W. Foley and music by Dr. Clarence Simeon Putnam

Entered the Union November 2, 1889, as the 39th state

Capital Bismarck

Population (2010 Census) 672,591 Ranked 48th state

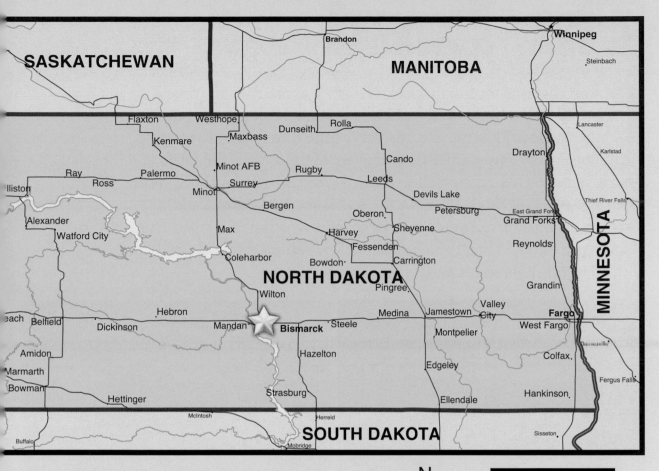

Map Scale

0   50 Miles

N

LEGEND

—	Road
—	River
☆	State Capital
●	City
▦	North Dakota
━	State Border

STATE CAPITAL

Bismarck served as the capital of the Dakota Territory from 1883 to 1889. It became a state capital when North Dakota was admitted to the Union in 1889. The **capitol** is sometimes called the "Skyscraper on the Prairie." The building is just over 241 feet tall, but it stands out in the area. The capitol was completed in 1934. The original building was destroyed by fire in 1930.

United States

Hawai'i   Alaska   **North Dakota**

The Land

From east to west the surface of North Dakota rises in three broad steps. In the west is an area of high, level ground called the Missouri Plateau. Because very little rain falls in the region, farming is nearly impossible. In the center of the state is the Drift Prairie region. This gently rolling plain is covered with **pothole lakes**. The rich soil is ideal farmland. In the east is the Red River Valley. This region was once covered by a large lake, which had formed from glacial meltwater. When the lake dried it left behind a treeless, flat land with rich soil. This soil is perfect for farming.

BADLANDS

The badlands are a dry area in the southwestern corner of the state where the land has been cut into unusual shapes by wind and water.

WHEAT FIELDS

North Dakota grows the vast majority of U.S. durum wheat. It has been said that the amount of durum wheat produced in the state each year is equal to 93 servings of pasta for each American.

RED RIVER

The Red River forms the border between North Dakota and Minnesota. It is sometimes called the Red River of the North.

LITTLE MISSOURI NATIONAL GRASSLANDS

The Little Missouri National Grasslands are near Bowman. The grasslands are one of three national grasslands in the state.

An Alberta clipper brings steep drops in temperature. An Alberta clipper happens after a low-pressure system in Alberta, Canada, causes warming there. The warmth mixes with a cold air mass and develops into a storm. The storm hits the jet stream, which quickly delivers the cold to North Dakota and other places where the jet stream travels.

Climate

N orth Dakota is one of the drier states in the country. Some areas in the northwest receive only 13 inches of rain or snow each year. The state's average precipitation is 17 inches per year.

The coldest temperature ever recorded in North Dakota was –60° Fahrenheit. It occurred on February 15, 1936, in Parshall. Later in the same year, the temperature reached a high of 121° F in Steele. North Dakota winters are long and very cold, while summers are short but hot. Temperatures at Bismarck can vary widely, because of the jet stream, which is a fast-moving air flow caused by the spinning of the planet. In July the temperatures are typically around 85° F. In January they often dip below 0° F.

Average Annual Temperatures Across North Dakota

Temperatures recorded around North Dakota typically show a wide range over the year, but the average annual temperature hovers around 40° F. Why do you think the temperature average tends to be similar in all parts of the state?

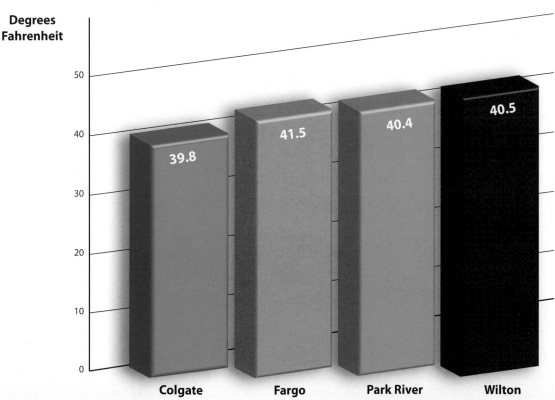

The American Wind Energy Association has declared that North Dakota has the greatest wind power potential of all the states. The state government is trying to attract investors to build additional wind turbines for electricity production. The state's current wind farms are advertised as visitor attractions.

Natural Resources

North Dakota's most important natural resource is, perhaps, its soil. In the Drift Prairie and Red River Valley regions, melting glaciers left behind layers of drift. This was a mixture of clay, sand, **humus**, and gravel that combined over time to form rich, dark soil.

Oil was discovered in the northwestern part of the state in 1951. The Williston Basin, located in western North Dakota, is rich with oil. The basin has a vast underground formation, called the Bakken Formation.

At first the oil was reached primarily by drills that dig straight down. Now, drills that access oil reserves from the side can be used. When the Garrison Dam was completed on the Missouri River in 1954, a huge reservoir known as Lake Sakakawea was formed. When crude oil and natural gas were discovered under Lake Sakakawea, it was tapped using drills that work horizontally.

Oil has been an important natural resource for North Dakotans. However, the state also contains large deposits of coal. North Dakota has one of the world's largest deposits of lignite coal. In the late 1800s, lignite coal was mined for heating and for running steam locomotives. Today, much of the coal that is mined is used to generate electricity.

Rich North Dakota farmland yields more than half of the nation's pinto beans. The state also grows 95 percent of U.S. flaxseed.

I DIDN'T KNOW THAT!

An energy plant built near Beulah converts lignite coal into a substitute for natural gas. It was the first plant built in the United States to make that kind of gas on a commercial scale.

Garrison Dam has several uses. It was built for flood control, and it was equipped with turbines that deliver hydroelectric power to several thousand customers.

North Dakota recognizes its dependence on its soil. The motto "Strength from the Soil" can be found on the state coat of arms and on the governor's flag.

North Dakotans have a state soil, known as Williams soil.

The state has many aquifers, which are natural pools of underground water, called groundwater. Some of this water is pumped to the surface and used for drinking. Many of the aquifers are under farmland, which uses agricultural chemicals that can seep through the soil into the groundwater. North Dakota is monitoring the groundwater in order to ensure that it stays safe to drink.

Plants

The majority of the land in North Dakota is considered prairie. The grasses are at their height in spring. The grasses are usually **dormant** during the summer, when there is little moisture. The roots of the grasses help keep the soil in place, which is why some of the prairies are protected.

Grass is not the only natural growth in the prairies. In the summer North Dakota's prairies are covered with flowers such as pasque flowers, black-eyed Susans, red lilies, and wild prairie roses. Berry pickers can find chokecherries, highbush cranberries, and wild plums.

Trees and bushes line the North Dakota landscape, mainly along rivers and streams. The state tree, the American elm, grows in river valleys. This tree can grow to be more than 100 feet tall. There are relatively few trees in North Dakota overall, however. Less than 1 percent of the state is forested.

AMERICAN ELM

The American elm usually flowers from March to May in North Dakota. It then grows round fruit called samaras.

PINCUSHION CACTUS

The pincushion cactus likes warm, dry areas where animals graze and keep the land clear of grasses.

BLACK-EYED SUSAN

The black-eyed Susan is a biennial flower, which means it flowers at the end of its second growing season. It is part of the sunflower family.

WHITE FRINGED ORCHID

The only threatened plant growing in North Dakota is the Great Plains white fringed orchid. It is federally protected because it is becoming rare.

The North Dakota Parks and Recreation Department offers, online, checklists of plants that nature lovers can look for when visiting the state parks.

One of the shrubs native to North Dakota is the early wild rose. Its pink flowers bloom in summer. The roses have been used for candy and sauces, for tea, and for perfume. The plant's oil has been used in medicines.

North Dakota grows nearly all of the U.S. canola. The canola plants are not native to North America, but they grow well in the state.

Researchers for the state study the effects of the fire on the vegetation and on the wildlife that lives in the grasslands. They research which plant species come back the fastest, in order to help deal with emergencies.

Animals

Prairie dogs, mule deer, and pronghorn antelope roam the badlands of North Dakota. White-tailed deer live throughout the state. Badgers, beavers, bobcats, and coyotes also call North Dakota home.

North Dakota has many different kinds of birds, including more breeding ducks than most states. Chase Lake National Wildlife Refuge, near Medina, has North America's largest breeding colony of white pelicans. The sandhill crane, a close relative of the whooping crane, is a migrating bird that lives in North Dakota in the fall.

The state's waters have many species of fish, including catfish, trout, perch, and bass. There are two federal fish hatcheries, which stock many lakes and rivers. Frogs, toads, turtles, and snakes, including the poisonous prairie rattlesnake, are among the state's reptiles.

FLICKERTAIL SQUIRREL

The flickertail squirrel, also called the Richardson's ground squirrel, makes its home in the state's central region.

WESTERN GREBE

Grebes are freshwater birds built for diving. Five species of grebes live in North Dakota, including the western grebe.

AMERICAN ELK

The elk has a different coat for warm and cold seasons. Its summer coat is deep reddish brown. Its winter coat is gray and brown.

BEAVER

Beavers live in and around water in lodges built from branches or whatever materials are nearby. Despite the cold North Dakota winters, the animals do not hibernate.

The red-throated loon is one of two species of loon that are native to North Dakota. Although they look like ducks, these birds are actually unrelated to ducks.

The only naturally occurring flock of whooping cranes **migrates** across North Dakota in spring and fall. The whooping crane is the tallest bird in North America and one of the rarest.

Tourism

Visitors can explore more than a dozen state parks and recreational areas, as well as several state forests and national grasslands. Theodore Roosevelt National Park is near Medora. The International Peace Garden, located on the Canadian border, attracts more than 150,000 visitors each year.

North Dakota offers many historical attractions. Tourists can walk through a restored pioneer town at Bonanzaville, near Fargo, or visit Fort Abercrombie, which was the first U.S. military post in North Dakota. Visitors can follow the route of explorers Meriwether Lewis and William Clark by taking a 300-mile drive along the banks of the Missouri River. The drive includes stops at a re-creation of Fort Mandan and at the Knife River Indian Villages National Historic Site.

THEODORE ROOSEVELT NATIONAL PARK

Theodore Roosevelt National Park is a 70,448-acre wildlife preserve in western North Dakota. At least 400 species of plants have been identified in the park.

FRONTIER VILLAGE

The world's largest bison statue is in the Frontier Village at Jamestown. It is 26 feet high and weighs 60 tons. In 2010, the statue was named Dakota Thunder in a contest that drew 3,565 entries.

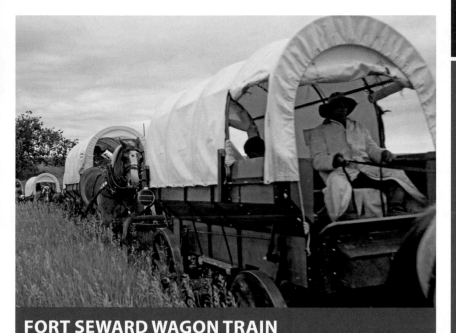

FORT SEWARD WAGON TRAIN

Events honoring pioneer life include the Fort Seward Wagon Train, a week-long adventure in which participants ride in a wagon train.

ROUGHRIDER 4 X 4 RENDEZVOUS

Annual events include the Roughrider 4 x 4 Rendezvous. In July, Watford City hosts 4 x 4 enthusiasts who explore the badlands in their vehicles. The event features a community bonfire and barbecue.

I DIDN'T KNOW THAT!

The International Peace Garden features the 120-foot-tall Peace Tower and the Peace Chapel. The floral displays in the garden change throughout the year, but floral flags of the United States and Canada are on display all year.

Theodore Roosevelt National Park was named after the 26th president of the United States. Roosevelt was a rancher in the Dakota Territory for several years after his first wife died. During that time, he lived in a small cabin. In 1886 he returned to the East, and he remarried.

North Dakota has fishing tournaments and derbies throughout the year, including several notable ice-fishing events. But the most competitive fishing is for walleye. The governor holds an annual championship that attracts hundreds of teams of serious fishers.

Industry

Agriculture has long been important to the state's economy. In addition to wheat, North Dakota's farmers also produce beans, barley, sunflowers, and flaxseed. Mining has a history nearly as long. The western part of the state yields coal and natural gas. Sulfur, krypton, ammonia, and other byproducts are recovered when the natural gas is processed. Valuable materials such as agates and flint are also collected. However, most employment comes from service industries, such as health care and financial services.

Industries in North Dakota
Value of Goods and Services in Millions of Dollars

In North Dakota, education accounts for only about one percent of the economy. This relates directly to the number of people and schools. Which other sectors relate directly to the number of people in the state?

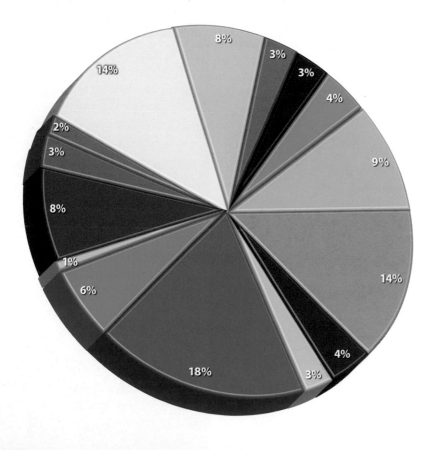

LEGEND

Agriculture, Forestry, and Fishing	$2,686
Mining	$977
Utilities	$874
Construction	$1,449
Manufacturing	$2,743
Wholesale and Retail Trade	$4,407
Transportation	$1,375
Media and Entertainment	$1,125
Finance, Insurance, and Real Estate	$5,618
Professional and Technical Services	$1,876
Education	$116
Health Care	$2,661
Hotels and Restaurants	$841
Other Services	$756
Government	$4,366
TOTAL	**$31,870**

Construction and manufacturing also make significant contributions to the economy. Most of the state's manufacturing is based on the processing of raw materials from farms. Wheat is made into breads and pastas, milk is used for cheeses, and sugar is extracted from sugar beets. Meatpacking plants produce steaks and sausages.

North Dakota is the fourth-largest oil producer among the states. Many North Dakotans are employed to drill for oil and to refine it. However, as in other states, North Dakota's service industries, such as health care and financial services, are now employing the majority of the state's workers.

North Dakota is a top producer of certified organic grain crops. Organic farms follow certain rules and use production practices that limit the use of chemicals.

I DIDN'T KNOW THAT!

A plant in Rolla uses artificial rubies and sapphires to create jewel **bearings**. The bearings made in Rolla are tiny, rounded objects that spin within machines. The bearings are used in watches and in U.S. military equipment.

North Dakota manufacturers make construction machinery, farm machinery, and products for computers and aircraft.

The pumps that remove oil from the ground are called "nodding donkeys."

Petroleum is the most important product mined in the state.

Lignite, found in the state's western half, is mined from the surface, by digging an open pit, and not from underground.

Goods and Services

North Dakota is a leading producer of numerous food crops. The crops are grown mainly in the Drift Prairie and Red River Valley regions, in the central and eastern parts of the state. But the economic benefit is felt throughout the state.

North Dakota ranks first in the nation in the production of sunflowers.

The U.S. Air Force has bases at Minot and Grand Forks, which employ thousands of workers. Minot Air Force Base was opened in the 1950s to protect the United States from missile attacks.

In recent years Kansas has grown more wheat, but North Dakota has long been the nation's leading producer of a certain type of high-protein wheat, called durum. This wheat variety is dense, which makes it suitable for pasta. North Dakota also has been the country's number-one producer of barley, as well as of flaxseed. The state has been among the leaders in rye and oat production. The state's sugar beets are a source of sugar, and its potatoes are made into potato chips and flakes for instant mashed potatoes, among other products.

Cattle are another important source of agricultural income in North Dakota. Cattle graze on ranches in the dry western part of the state. The cattle provide beef and dairy products. The state's farmers also raise hogs and sheep.

I DIDN'T KNOW THAT!

The Bank of North Dakota is based in Bismarck. North Dakota is the only state with a bank that is part of the state government.

The state bank is not backed by the U.S. government, as most banks in the United States are. It is backed by the people of North Dakota. The profits that the bank makes go to the state government.

The state is among the nation's leading producers of honey.

The prices of wheat and oil can vary greatly. Price increases and reductions can have a dramatic effect on the state's income.

The North Dakota Stockmen's Association has three licensed law enforcement officers who investigate modern cases of cattle rustling. Hundreds of brand inspectors work at the livestock markets, checking to make sure the right ranchers are credited for owning the right cows.

American Indians

People have lived for thousands of years on the land that is now North Dakota. Early North Dakotans hunted big game animals such as bison. After the hunters of bison came farmers who grew corn and squash.

By the time the first European visitors arrived in the 1700s and 1800s, a number of American Indian groups had settled near the Missouri River. They included the Mandan, the Hidatsa, and the Arikara. They built permanent villages, farmed the land, and hunted bison.

Among the other native peoples of North Dakota are the Dakota, or Dakota Sioux, who came from central Minnesota and settled in the Drift Prairie region, in the eastern part of the state. The Ojibwe, also from Minnesota, moved into the forests of the Turtle and Pembina mountains of the north-central and northeastern regions. The Cree and the Assiniboine also lived in the northeast. These groups remained in the area until conflicts over land developed with the U.S. government during the second half of the 1800s.

Bison were important to the American Indians. Bison meat was used for food, and the hides and bones were used to make shelters, clothes, boats, and tools.

In the 1820s and later, U.S. traders gave American Indians metal pots, axes, and other items in exchange for furs. The traders also brought diseases that the American Indians had not encountered before. In 1837, the Mandan population was reduced from about 1,600 people to about 130 people by an outbreak of smallpox and cholera.

The Dakota were one of the larger American Indian groups in North Dakota. The Dakota, Lakota, and Nakota are divisions of the Sioux.

I DIDN'T KNOW THAT!

Many French fur traders married American Indian women. Their children were called the Métis.

Migrating American Indians, such as the Dakota, lived in tepees. The portable structures are also known as tipis or teepees.

To say "hello" the Assiniboine and Sioux say, "Hau." Their greeting is said the way "how" is pronounced. The Ojibwe say, "Boozhoo." The Hidatsa say, "Dosha."

After the 1837 smallpox epidemic, the Mandan, Arikara, and Hidatsa banded together in order to survive. They became known as the "three affiliated tribes."

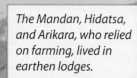
The Mandan, Hidatsa, and Arikara, who relied on farming, lived in earthen lodges.

Explorers and Missionaries

It is believed that no person of European heritage set foot in North Dakota until 1738. In that year, Pierre Gaultier de Varennes, sieur de La Vérendrye, a French Canadian fur trader, encountered the Mandan people. He was followed by other fur traders from France, Great Britain, and Spain. The fur trade soon came under the control of two British-owned companies. Their names were the North West Company and the Hudson's Bay Company.

In 1801 the first permanent trading post in North Dakota was established at Pembina by Alexander Henry the Younger of the North West Company. In 1803, under President Thomas Jefferson, the United States bought from France a large land parcel called the Louisiana Purchase. The new land included most of what is now North Dakota. Soon after, Jefferson sent Meriwether Lewis and William Clark to explore the new American territory. Lewis and Clark passed the winter of 1804–1805 with the Mandan people in what is now North Dakota.

In the 1800s, a small number of missionaries also ventured into the area. The first of these was a Catholic priest, Sévère Dumoulin, who built a chapel at Pembina in 1818. That same year Father Joseph Provencher started a mission at Fort Douglas. Catholic missionary Father George Anthony Belcourt built the state's first flour mill at St. Joseph in 1851.

Timeline of Settlement

Early Explorers and Traders

1738 Pierre Gaultier de Varennes, sieur de La Vérendrye, visits the American Indians living near what is now Bismarck.

1790s Fur traders from Canada are frequent visitors to the North Dakota area.

1790s John Evans, an explorer from Wales, travels the area in search of a legendary tribe of Welsh-speaking Indians. Instead he finds the Mandan people.

1797 David Thompson, an English **surveyor**, surveys part of North Dakota.

First Settlements

1801 Alexander Henry the Younger establishes the first long-term trading post in Pembina.

1803 The United States makes the Louisiana Purchase. Soon afterward, Meriwether Lewis and William Clark explore the region. Their reports attract fur traders to the area.

1818 Father Sévère Dumoulin, a Catholic priest, builds a chapel at Pembina. That same year, the first school opens in Pembina.

Territory and Statehood

1861 The U.S. government establishes the Dakota Territory, including the land that is now both North and South Dakota. Americans from the East and European **immigrants** begin arriving to stake land claims.

1862 The U.S. Congress passes the Homestead Act, giving free land in the West, including what is now North Dakota, to people who will farm it. A rush of new settlers moves into the region.

1889 In February, the remaining Dakota Territory is divided in two parts.

1889 In November, North Dakota and South Dakota are admitted to the Union. President Benjamin Harrison signs the documents making them separate states.

Early Settlers

In 1812 Scottish and Irish settlers came from Canada to start their own colony, called the Selkirk Colony. The settlers lived at Pembina and grew food for fur trappers and traders. They also started North Dakota's first school.

Map of Settlements and Resources in Early North Dakota

4 *In 1858 the first Fort Abercrombie is built on the Red River. After the Dakota Territory is established in 1861, the U.S. Army builds a number of forts for the territory.*

5 *From 1875 to 1890, investors buy huge areas of land in the Red River Valley. Large farms called bonanza farms are established.*

1 *In 1801, Alexander Henry the Younger builds a trading post at what is now Pembina.*

2 *In 1812, the Selkirk Colony is formed at Pembina. The settlers, who come from Canada, begin to farm the area.*

3 *The Red River Valley, in the east, is* **ceded** *to the United States by the British in 1818. Fur trading begins to boom in the eastern part of the state.*

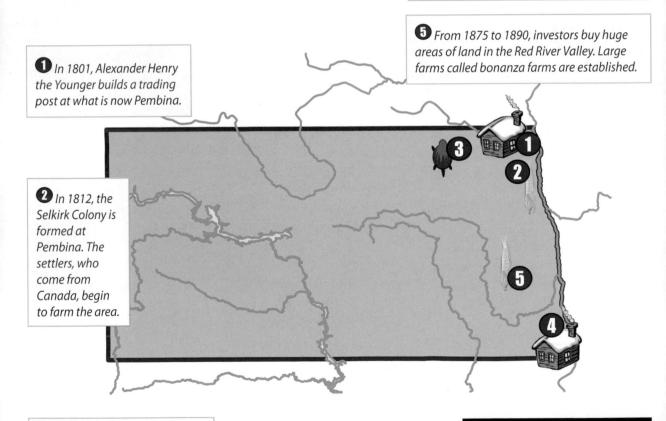

N

Scale
0   50 Miles

LEGEND	
Settlement	Farming
River	North Dakota
Fur	State Border

The flow of settlers increased in the 1860s, after the Dakota Territory was created and the land was opened up for **homesteading**. As settlement increased, conflicts arose between the settlers and the original inhabitants. Eventually the United States forced many American Indians onto **reservations**.

Some Americans and European immigrants decided against moving to the new Dakota Territory because of the conflicts with the American Indians. Drought, prairie fires, and blizzards ravaged the area from time to time. This also discouraged settlers. Transportation was a problem, too. Although there were steamboats on the Missouri and Red rivers, an overland journey by stagecoach or ox-drawn wagon was difficult and dangerous. When the first railroad came to the area in 1872, travel became much easier. As transportation improved, settlement increased.

The Homestead Act of 1862 offered free land to anyone willing to live on it and farm it for five years. The Timber Culture Act of 1873 also offered cheap land to settlers.

Notable People

Many people from North Dakota have made a mark on U.S. history. North Dakotans were making important contributions and influencing American thought when the state was still part of the Dakota Territory. The state's leaders have excelled in the many arenas of life, from politics to military service.

SITTING BULL
(1831–1890)

Sitting Bull was a Lakota chief. After gold was discovered in the Dakota Territory, the U.S. government began to force the area's American Indians onto reservations. He led the fight to keep the land. In 1877, Sitting Bull led his people to Canada and did not give up until 1881. Back in the United States, he was a performer for a short time in Buffalo Bill's Wild West Show. Afterward, he moved onto a reservation. In 1890, Lakota police arrested him because the reservation authorities feared he would lead an uprising. In the gunfight that followed, he was killed.

THEODORE ROOSEVELT
(1858–1919)

Theodore Roosevelt was elected to the New York legislature right after college. When his first wife died, he left the East and invested in cattle ranching in North Dakota. By 1889, he was remarried and serving on the U.S. Civil Service Commission. He later served as New York City police commissioner and as the assistant secretary of the U.S. Navy. He fought in the Spanish-American War, was elected governor of New York, and served as the U.S. vice president. Roosevelt became president when President William McKinley was assassinated in 1901. He was elected to another term as president in 1904.

ERIC SEVAREID
(1912–1992)

Born in Velva, young Eric Sevareid was a protégé of Edward R. Morrow, the famous radio journalist. Sevareid reported from Paris; London; Washington, D.C.; and Asia during World War II. He later served as chief Washington correspondent for CBS-TV and moderated numerous news programs.

DAVID CHARLES JONES
(1921–)

David C. Jones went to high school and college in North Dakota. He entered the Army Air Corps in 1942. During World War II, he was a flight instructor and training officer. After combat in Korea and Vietnam, he rose to commander of U.S. Air Forces in Europe, then the chairman of the Joint Chiefs of Staff.

WARREN CHRISTOPHER
(1925– 2011)

Born in Scranton, Warren Christopher was the deputy attorney general under President Lyndon Johnson and deputy secretary of state under President Jimmy Carter. President Bill Clinton appointed him secretary of state. In Clinton's Cabinet, he helped negotiate a Middle East peace agreement.

I DIDN'T KNOW THAT!

James Buchli (1945–) was born in New Rockford and graduated from Fargo High School. He entered the U.S. Naval Academy, served in Vietnam with the Marines, and then entered flight training. In 1979, he became an astronaut. In four space flights, he orbited Earth 319 times.

Phil Jackson (1945–) attended high school in Williston and played basketball for the University of North Dakota. He played professionally for the New York Knicks and New Jersey Nets but achieved his greatest success as a coach for the Chicago Bulls and Los Angeles Lakers. Jackson has won 11 championships, more than any other coach in the history of the National Basketball Association.

Population

North Dakota ranks 48th among the 50 states in total population. The 2010 U.S. Census found that fewer than 673,000 people lived in North Dakota. Only Vermont and Wyoming had smaller populations. Because of its fairly large land area, North Dakota is one of only a few states to have fewer than 10 people per square mile of land. For the United States as a whole, the **population density** is more than 87 people per square mile.

The state of North Dakota keeps track of counties in which the population is fewer than six people per square mile. They are called frontier counties, and more than half of the counties in the state qualify. However, North Dakota's cities, while small by national standards, are getting larger. Fargo, with about 96,000 people, is the state's largest city. Bismarck, with about 61,000 people, and Grand Forks, with about 51,000, are the other cities with populations over 50,000.

North Dakota Population 1950–2010

North Dakota's population has increased in most decades since 1950, but overall, the population growth has been slow. What factors may have kept North Dakota's population from growing at a faster rate?

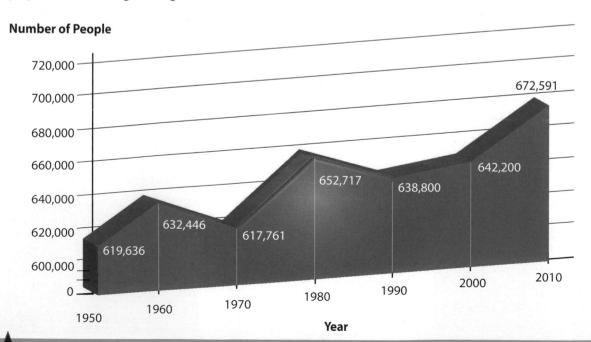

Number of People

The North Dakota college and university system has 11 campuses, including North Dakota State University and the University of North Dakota.

North Dakota is the only state in which citizens do not need to register before voting. The state relies on its small precincts to make sure that the people who vote really live in the precincts.

About one-fifth of the population of North Dakota is under the age of 18.

Out of every 50 people in North Dakota, only one was born outside the United States.

Fargo, North Dakota's largest city, has a twin city in Minnesota, called Moorhead. The metropolitan area is known as Fargo-Moorhead.

The grounds of the capitol in Bismarck feature a statue of a pioneer family, a heritage center, the state library, and the governor's residence.

Politics and Government

T he state's government is divided into three branches. As in other states, these branches are the legislative, the executive, and the judicial branches. The legislative branch, called the Legislative Assembly, makes the laws. It is made up of a Senate with 47 members and a House of Representatives with 94 members. Legislators are elected to four-year terms.

The executive branch carries out the laws. The governor is the chief executive and is elected to a four-year term. The state also elects a lieutenant governor and several other officials. A number of officials are appointed.

The judicial branch interprets the laws by ruling on civil and criminal cases. The highest court is the Supreme Court, which is made up of five judges who are called justices. They are elected to ten-year terms. District court judges in North Dakota are elected to six-year terms.

The North Dakota State Library manages a network of online resources that are helpful for people in rural areas. This includes an online form that residents can use to ask a librarian to look up information for them.

Cultural Groups

About 90 percent of North Dakota's residents can trace their roots back to European countries. Early Norwegian settlers established themselves in the Red River Valley and in north-central North Dakota. Many Germans and Russians settled in the south-central part of the state. In 1890, North Dakota had a higher percentage of people who were born in other countries than any other state.

North Dakotans of Scandinavian heritage celebrate their culture at Fargo's Scandinavian Hjemkomst Festival. *Hjemkomst* means "homecoming." The event has attracted members of the Norwegian royal family to North Dakota.

Drumming is an important aspect of the American Indian powwows held in the state. The United Tribes International Powwow, for example, features more than 1,500 dancers, singers, and drummers.

Oom-pah music is a central part of Oktoberfest festivities. It is also known as oompah or umpapa music. Tubas play the main part of the chords, or the "oom." The "pah" is played by accordions or other instruments.

German culture is honored at the state's numerous Oktoberfest celebrations. The town of New Leipzig is sometimes called the "Small, Friendly German Town on the Dakota Prairie." Each fall New Leipzig hosts a traditional German Oktoberfest. Fargo hosts an annual German Folk Festival in the summer. The German Folk Festival is a celebration of German music, traditional clothing, and food.

The largest non-European cultural group in the state is American Indians. They number about 6 percent of the population. Many American Indians live on reservations. The Mandan, Hidatsa, and Arikara are based at Fort Berthold. The Turtle Mountain Reservation is home to the Turtle Mountain Band of Ojibwe. Many Sioux live at the Devils Lake Sioux Reservation. Other divisions of the Sioux occupy the Lake Traverse and Standing Rock reservations, both of which are partly in South Dakota.

The city of Minot is home to the Norsk Høstfest. It is North America's largest Scandinavian festival. The event features world-class entertainment and includes traditional Scandinavian foods.

Knife River Indian Villages, in Stanton, is a national historic site where prehistoric American Indian culture is preserved.

The name of the Norwegian American celebration in Minot was changed from Norsk Hostefest to Norsk Høstfest after people pointed out that *Hostefest* means "Coughing Festival" and not "Harvest Festival" as intended.

Wild horses that run free in the Theodore Roosevelt National Park have been traced to Spanish ponies and to American Indian horses. Indian groups are working in partnership with others to save and promote the native horses.

Arts and Entertainment

North Dakota holds dozens of festivals each year. The North Dakota State Fair at Minot takes place in July, and the Dakota Cowboy Poetry Gathering is held annually in Medora. The North Dakota Winter Show takes place in Valley City every March.

At any time of year, residents and visitors can enjoy the state's museums, art galleries, zoos, and dance companies. The Trollwood Performing Arts School puts on full-length musicals. The Children's Museum at Yunker Farm offers families hands-on exhibits about nature and agriculture. Young visitors can observe live bees in a giant honeycomb and then crawl through a model of a honeycomb made to fit people. In Dickinson, the Dakota Dinosaur Museum features **fossils**.

Visitors to the Dakota Dinosaur Museum can view full-scale dinosaur replicas. The museum's large collection of fossils was started in 1984, when dinosaur remains were dug out of the ground nearby.

Music lovers can attend performances by symphony orchestras in Minot, Fargo, and Grand Forks. The annual International Old Time Fiddlers Contest occurs at the International Peace Garden.

Well-known artists and performers have come from North Dakota. Maxwell Anderson, a graduate of the University of North Dakota, was a Pulitzer Prize–winning playwright. Louis L'Amour, a writer of best-selling Western novels, grew up in Jamestown. North Dakotan Lawrence Welk became a popular bandleader with his own long-running television show. Angie Dickinson acted in movies and starred in the 1970s television series *Police Woman*. Phyllis Frelich, an actor who is deaf, was a founding member of the National Theatre of the Deaf.

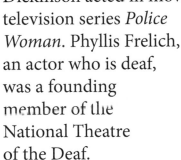

The movie Fargo *was set in North Dakota and was partly filmed in the state. The film won Academy Awards for its screenwriters and for Frances McDormand as best actress.*

I DIDN'T KNOW THAT!

The state's universities and colleges are important cultural centers. North Dakota State University is home to the Reineke Visual Arts Gallery.

Every year the town of Turtle Lake hosts the USA National Championship Turtle Races. Activities include a soapbox derby, a softball tournament, street dancing, and the turtle race itself.

North Dakota native Richard Edlund collected several Academy Awards for his special-effects work in movies such as *Star Wars* and *Raiders of the Lost Ark*.

Medora hosts an annual festival of cowboy poetry. This type of verse celebrates ranching and is traditionally shared by spoken word.

Sports

While there are no major league sports teams in North Dakota, residents enjoy watching college and high school sports, especially basketball and football. These sporting events and their hometown heroes are covered by local media, such as radio and television stations.

North Dakota is host to many sports events. The Prairie Rose State Games has competitive events similar to the Olympics. The town of Sentinel Butte hosts the Champions Ride Rodeo every August. Potato Bowl USA in Grand Forks is another popular gathering. It takes place in September and features a football game and a parade.

Summertime activities in North Dakota include biking, golf, fishing, and hunting. Lake Sakakawea is popular among water-skiers, boaters, swimmers, and scuba divers.

Baseball great Roger Maris grew up in North Dakota. He was voted the American League's Most Valuable Player in 1960 and again in 1961, when he hit 61 home runs, the major league record at that time.

Devils Lake, with its three park and recreation areas, is also a popular destination. Lake Metigoshe State Park attracts picnickers and campers. Theodore Roosevelt National Park brings in campers, bird-watchers, and history buffs.

North Dakota's winter sports make the most of the cold, snowy weather. Many outdoor enthusiasts set out on cross-country skis, snowmobiles, snowshoes, or sleds. Many lakes are open for ice fishing. People can lace up their skates to exercise on indoor and outdoor rinks. Skaters can take part in hockey games. Teams also take to the ice for the sport of curling. In curling, the players slide heavy stones toward a target across the ice.

The games of the North Dakota State Bison and University of North Dakota Fighting Sioux attract many fans from outside the universities.

I DIDN'T KNOW THAT!

Portal has an international golf course that stretches into Canada. The tee for the ninth hole is in Canada, and the cup is in the United States.

The Killdeer Mountain Roundup Rodeo is the oldest professional rodeo in North Dakota.

The University of North Dakota's men's hockey team, the Fighting Sioux, has won seven national championships and nine conference championships. They won their first national championship in 1958.

Boxer Virgil Hill grew up in North Dakota. Hill won championships in the light heavyweight and cruiser weight divisions.

North Dakota has more golf holes per capita than any other state. This includes the nine holes at Bois de Sioux Golf Club. At that club, there are nine holes in North Dakota and nine holes in Minnesota.

National Averages Comparison

T he United States is a federal republic, consisting of fifty states and the District of Columbia. Alaska and Hawai'i are the only non-contiguous, or non-touching, states in the nation. Today, the United States of America is the third-largest country in the world in population. The United States Census Bureau takes a census, or count of all the people, every ten years. It also regularly collects other kinds of data about the population and the economy. How does North Dakota compare to the national average?

Comparison Chart

United States 2010 Census Data *	USA	North Dakota
Admission to Union	NA	November 2, 1889
Land Area (in square miles)	3,537,438.44	68,975.93
Population Total	308,745,538	672,591
Population Density (people per square mile)	87.28	9.75
Population Percentage Change (April 1, 2000, to April 1, 2010)	9.7%	4.7%
White Persons (percent)	72.4%	90.0%
Black Persons (percent)	12.6%	1.2%
American Indian and Alaska Native Persons (percent)	0.9%	5.4%
Asian Persons (percent)	4.8%	1.0%
Native Hawaiian and Other Pacific Islander Persons (percent)	0.2%	—
Some Other Race (percent)	6.2%	0.5%
Persons Reporting Two or More Races (percent)	2.9%	1.8%
Persons of Hispanic or Latino Origin (percent)	16.3%	2.0%
Not of Hispanic or Latino Origin (percent)	83.7%	98.0%
Median Household Income	$52,029	$45,996
Percentage of People Age 25 or Over Who Have Graduated from High School	80.4%	83.9%

*All figures are based on the 2010 United States Census, with the exception of the last two items. Percentages may not add to 100 because of rounding.

How to Improve My Community

Strong communities make strong states. Think about what features are important in your community. What do you value? Education? Health? Forests? Safety? Beautiful spaces? Government works to help citizens create ideal living conditions that are fair to all by providing services in communities. Consider what changes you could make in your community. How would they improve your state as a whole? Using this concept web as a guide, write a report that outlines the features you think are most important in your community and what improvements could be made. A strong state needs strong communities.

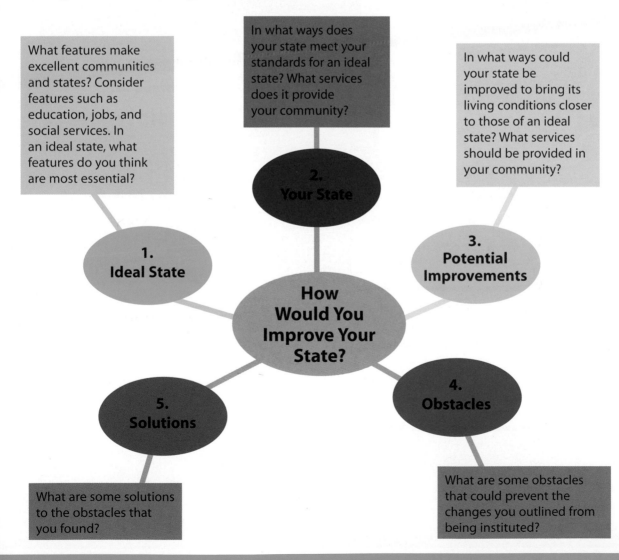

What features make excellent communities and states? Consider features such as education, jobs, and social services. In an ideal state, what features do you think are most essential?

In what ways does your state meet your standards for an ideal state? What services does it provide your community?

In what ways could your state be improved to bring its living conditions closer to those of an ideal state? What services should be provided in your community?

2. Your State

1. Ideal State

3. Potential Improvements

How Would You Improve Your State?

5. Solutions

4. Obstacles

What are some solutions to the obstacles that you found?

What are some obstacles that could prevent the changes you outlined from being instituted?

Exercise Your Mind!

Think about these questions and then use your research skills to find the answers and learn more fascinating facts about North Dakota. A teacher, librarian, or parent may be able to help you locate the best sources to use in your research.

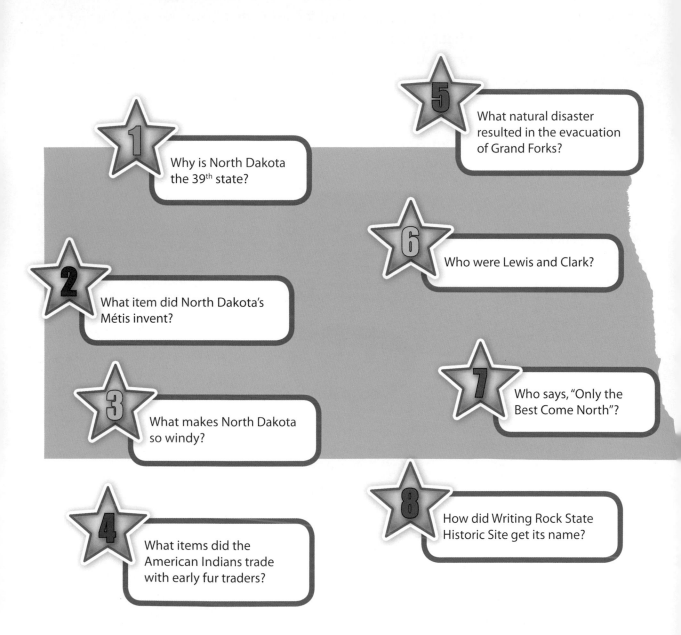

1 Why is North Dakota the 39th state?

2 What item did North Dakota's Métis invent?

3 What makes North Dakota so windy?

4 What items did the American Indians trade with early fur traders?

5 What natural disaster resulted in the evacuation of Grand Forks?

6 Who were Lewis and Clark?

7 Who says, "Only the Best Come North"?

8 How did Writing Rock State Historic Site get its name?

Words to Know

bearings: machine parts that support other moving parts, usually parts that rotate

capitol: the building for the legislature

ceded: transferred land by treaty

dormant: a condition or state of rest

fossils: the remains of prehistoric plants or animals

homesteading: developing farmland in order to be granted its ownership

humus: substance in dirt that comes from decaying plants or animals preserved in rock

immigrants: people who move to a place from another country

lignite: a soft type of coal with a woodlike texture

migrates: moves seasonally from one place to another

population density: the average number of people per unit or area

pothole lakes: small, shallow basins left behind by glaciers

reservations: lands set aside, or reserved, for American Indians

surveyor: someone who measures land

Index

Log on to www.av2books.com

AV² by Weigl brings you media enhanced books that support active learning. Go to www.av2books.com, and enter the special code found on page 2 of this book. You will gain access to enriched and enhanced content that supplements and complements this book. Content includes video, audio, web links, quizzes, a slide show, and activities.

Audio
Listen to sections of the book read aloud.

Video
Watch informative video clips.

Embedded Weblinks
Gain additional information for research.

Try This!
Complete activities and hands-on experiments.

WHAT'S ONLINE?

Try This!	Embedded Weblinks	Video	EXTRA FEATURES
Test your knowledge of the state in a mapping activity.	Discover more attractions in North Dakota.	Watch a video introduction to North Dakota.	**Audio** Listen to sections of the book read aloud.
Find out more about precipitation in your city.	Learn more about the history of the state.	Watch a video about the features of the state.	
Plan what attractions you would like to visit in the state.	Learn the full lyrics of the state song.		**Key Words** Study vocabulary, and complete a matching word activity.
Learn more about the early natural resources of the state.			
Write a biography about a notable resident of North Dakota.			**Slide Show** View images and captions, and prepare a presentation
Complete an educational census activity.			**Quizzes** Test your knowledge.

AV² was built to bridge the gap between print and digital. We encourage you to tell us what you like and what you want to see in the future.

Sign up to be an AV² Ambassador at www.av2books.com/ambassador.